Nashua Public Library

Enjoy this book!

Please remember to return it on time
so that others may enjoy it too.

Manage your library account and
discover all we offer by visiting us
online at www.nashualibrary.org

Love your library? Tell a friend!

COUNTRY PROFILES

ITALY

BY AMY RECHNER

BLASTOFF!
DISCOVERY

BELLWETHER MEDIA • MINNEAPOLIS, MN

Blastoff! Discovery launches a new mission: reading to learn. Filled with facts and features, each book offers you an exciting new world to explore!

This edition first published in 2018 by Bellwether Media, Inc.

No part of this publication may be reproduced in whole or in part without written permission of the publisher.
For information regarding permission, write to Bellwether Media, Inc., Attention: Permissions Department,
5357 Penn Avenue South, Minneapolis, MN 55419.

Library of Congress Cataloging-in-Publication Data

Names: Rechner, Amy, author.
Title: Italy / by Amy Rechner.
Description: Minneapolis, MN : Bellwether Media, Inc., [2018]
    | Series: Blastoff! Discovery: Country Profiles | Includes
    bibliographical references and index. | Audience: Grades
    3-8. | Audience: Ages 7-13.
Identifiers: LCCN 2016057458 (print) | LCCN 2016057540
    (ebook) | ISBN 9781626176836 (hardcover : alk. paper)
    | ISBN 9781681034133 (ebook)
Subjects: LCSH: Italy–Juvenile literature.
Classification: LCC DG417 .R43 2018 (print) | LCC DG417
    (ebook) | DDC 945–dc23
LC record available at https://lccn.loc.gov/2016057458

Editor: Christina Leaf   Designer: Brittany McIntosh

Printed in the United States of America, North Mankato, MN.

TABLE OF CONTENTS

THE COLOSSEUM
ROME

The sun blazes over the Eternal City of Rome. **Tourists** dodge traffic across busy streets to visit an ancient site. Before them stands the Colosseum, the world's largest **amphitheater**. Quiet descends as they walk through its stone arches.

OTHER TOP SITES

ANCIENT CITY OF POMPEII

LEANING TOWER OF PISA

FLORENCE DUOMO

THE GRAND CANAL

Tiered seats of stone, nearly two thousand years old, greet the visitors. Tourists look below to the Colosseum's center. **Gladiators**, animals, and others fought in the arena to amuse Romans and their emperors. Time and weather have taken a toll on the Colosseum, but it still remains. Ancient history stands strong in modern Italy!

5

LOCATION

Italy is a long, boot-shaped **peninsula** in southern Europe. France, Switzerland, Austria, and Slovenia share Italy's northern border. The Adriatic and Ionian Seas are east. The Tyrrhenian Sea lies to the southwest. Inside Italy are two tiny, independent nations. San Marino is one. It is in northern Italy. The other is Vatican City. It lies in central Italy, within the capital city, Rome.

Italy spans 116,348 square miles (301,340 square kilometers). This includes many islands. Sicily and Sardinia are the largest. Sicily lies near the toe of Italy's boot. Sardinia is west, in the Mediterranean Sea.

SWITZERLAND

FRANCE

TURIN

MEDITERRANEAN SEA

N
W E
S

AUSTRIA

VENICE

SLOVENIA

MILAN

SAN MARINO

FLORENCE

ADRIATIC
SEA

ROME

VATICAN
CITY

NAPLES

TYRRHENIAN
SEA

ITALY

SARDINIA

SEA MORE!

How many seas surround Italy?
The true answer is one! The
Tyrrhenian, Ionian, and Adriatic
Seas are all smaller bodies within
the larger Mediterranean Sea.

IONIAN
SEA

SICILY

PALERMO

Mountains and hills dominate Italy's **terrain**. The Alps mountain range lines the northern border. The Apennine Mountains cascade down the length of the country. Mount Etna in Sicily and Mount Vesuvius near Naples are active **volcanoes**. A large **plain** surrounds the Po, Italy's longest river. The Po flows east through northern Italy to the Adriatic Sea.

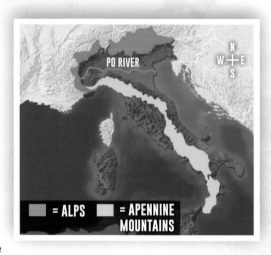

PO RIVER

N W+E S

= ALPS = APENNINE MOUNTAINS

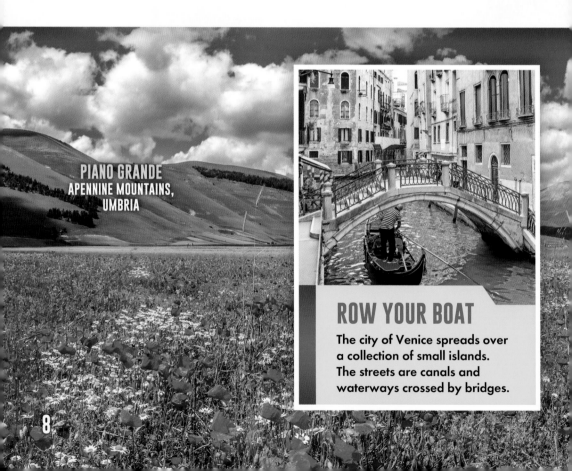

PIANO GRANDE
APENNINE MOUNTAINS, UMBRIA

ROW YOUR BOAT

The city of Venice spreads over a collection of small islands. The streets are canals and waterways crossed by bridges.

PO RIVER
PO VALLEY, PIEDMONT

ROME

Average
seasonal highs
and lows

JANUARY
HIGH: 55 °F (13 °C)
LOW: 37 °F (3 °C)

APRIL
HIGH: 66 °F (19 °C)
LOW: 46 °F (8 °C)

JULY
HIGH: 90 °F (32 °C)
LOW: 66 °F (19 °C)

OCTOBER
HIGH: 68 °F (20 °C)
LOW: 54 °F (12 °C)

°F = degrees Fahrenheit
°C = degrees Celsius

Most of Italy has a **temperate** climate. Summers
are warm. Winters are mild, with snow in the northern
mountains. The Po Valley gets rain in spring and fall.
The climate of southern Italy is hot and dry.

WILDLIFE

Much of Italy's wildlife lives in remote mountain regions. Lynx, marmots, and brown bears have been spotted in the Alps. A rare type of goat-like chamois grazes in the Apennine Mountains. Wolves, Italy's unofficial animal, also live and hunt in mountain regions. They are protected by Italy's government.

Red foxes, wild boars, and roe deer live in the woodlands. Pink flamingos stand tall in **lagoons**. Jellyfish, whales, and seals swim in the seas around Italy.

EURASIAN LYNX

MARMOT

WILD BOAR

MEDITERRANEAN JELLYFISH

CHAMOIS

ITALIAN WOLVES

ITALIAN WOLF

Life Span: 13 years
Red List Status: least concern

Italian wolf range =

LEAST CONCERN	NEAR THREATENED	VULNERABLE	ENDANGERED	CRITICALLY ENDANGERED	EXTINCT IN THE WILD	EXTINCT

GREETINGS

Ciao, pronounced CHOW, means both hello and goodbye in Italian. It is used when talking with friends. It has become so popular that people in other countries use it too!

Italy is home to 62 million people. The country's official language is Italian. There are hundreds of local languages spoken, too. It is common for people to speak both their **native** language and Italian. Some communities in northern Italy blend their Italian culture with the German and French influence of their neighboring countries. The islands of Sicily and Sardinia each have distinct cultures and languages. Italians take pride in their local **heritage**.

12

Four out of five Italians are Christian. Most of them are Catholic. There is also a small Muslim population. Many Italians do not practice any religion at all.

FAMOUS FACE
Name: Andrea Bocelli
Birthday: September 22, 1958
Hometown: Lajatico, Italy
Famous for: Blind singer who has crossed over into international success by blending opera with pop music

SPEAK ITALIAN

ENGLISH	ITALIAN	HOW TO SAY IT
hello	buon giorno	bwon JOR-no
goodbye	arrivederci	ah-ree-va-DAER-chee
please	per favore	pear fahv-OR-eh
thank you	grazie	GRAHT-zee-eh
yes	sì	see
no	no	no

VERONA

PIAZZA NAVONA
ROME

Italian families are close-knit. Extended families often share daily meals. Elders are treated with great respect. Italians are also involved with their communities. They meet and connect with friends and neighbors in public squares called *piazzas*. The piazza is often a daily stop in an Italian's life. Local culture and language are handed down through generations and shared at the piazza.

More Italians live in cities than small villages. City dwellers live in apartments. Single-family homes are becoming common in cities and the countryside. Often, adult children live with their parents until they can afford to buy a home.

CUSTOMS

Italian people are both formal and friendly. Strangers are greeted with a smile and a firm handshake. New friends meet in cafes or restaurants instead of homes. The formality is eventually replaced by a warm, informal affection. Close friends are greeted with kisses on each cheek and more casual language.

CAFE, ROME

#cuoredinapoli

When Italians have a conversation, they use more than just words. Hand gestures are a big part of the Italian way of speaking. The gestures help to emphasize what a person is trying to say.

Italian children must attend school until the age of 16. Most stay in school longer. They can choose to focus on specific areas like science or the arts, or train for certain jobs. Many students also go on to a university.

Most Italians work in **service jobs** such as tourism, banking, and information technology. Many other people work in manufacturing jobs to build machinery, automobiles, and textiles. Only a small number of Italians are farmers. They produce world-famous wine, olives, and grains.

WORKERS MAKING MASERATI CARS

FANCY PANTS

Italy is one of the best places to be for fashion! Some of the world's most famous designers of clothes and shoes are Italian. Milan is the heart of Italy's fashion world.

FALL FASHION WEEK 2017 MILAN

CALCIO

The most popular sport in Italy is *calcio*, known as soccer in the U.S. There are 20 clubs, or teams, in Italy's top soccer league. The Italian men's national soccer team has won the **World Cup** four times. Basketball and volleyball are popular sports, too. Northern Italy's Alps offer skiing, ice skating, and other sports in winter.

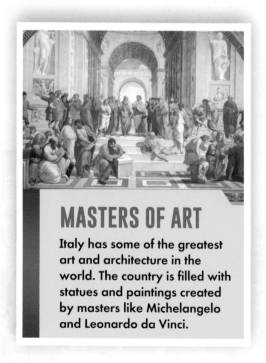

MASTERS OF ART

Italy has some of the greatest art and architecture in the world. The country is filled with statues and paintings created by masters like Michelangelo and Leonardo da Vinci.

Cycling is a serious sport in Italy. The mountainous terrain challenges the world's best cyclists in the *Giro d'Italia* each summer. For lovers of auto racing, Italy hosts the thrilling Italian Grand Prix.

GIRO D'ITALIA

MORRA

Morra is a quick-draw hand game that Italians have been playing since ancient Rome. At least two people are needed to play. The object is to guess how many fingers your opponent will show while they guess how many fingers you will show.

How to Play:

1. Two opponents and a referee stand or sit together. At a signal, opponents show a number of fingers on one hand. Any number, one through five, is acceptable.

2. As you show your hand, guess out loud the number of fingers your opponent will show. Your opponent will do the same thing at the same time.

3. If you are right, you get as many points as there are fingers shown. If you are both right or both wrong, no points are awarded. Whoever reaches 16 points first wins!

FOOD

SLOW FOOD

Meals are when Italian families and friends enjoy time together. Food is carefully prepared and eaten slowly. It can take hours to enjoy an Italian dinner.

Some of the world's favorite foods come from Italy! Pizza was invented in Naples. Italian pizza is very different from the American kind, with less cheese and thinner crusts. Pasta is another favorite from Italy, although it is rarely served as a main dish. Italian **cuisine** showcases the country's fresh vegetables, grains, and olive oil.

Italy's main meals have three parts. Dinner begins with a small portion of pasta, soup, or *risotto*, a rice dish. The main course comes next and is usually meat or fish. Side dishes of vegetables or salad may be served with it or afterwards. The meal ends with dessert, such as **gelato**, cake, or simple *biscotti* cookies.

RISOTTO
GELATO

NUTELLA AND BERRY BRUSCHETTA RECIPE

Bruschetta is an Italian dish usually consisting of bread topped with olive oil and tomatoes. This variation features Nutella, a spread invented in the Piedmont region.

Ingredients:
1 long French bread cut into
   1/2-inch thick slices
1 cup blackberries or raspberries
   (fresh or frozen, thawed)
1 teaspoon orange juice
Nutella Hazelnut Spread

Steps:
1. In a bowl, soak the berries in orange juice.
2. Toast bread slices until golden. Spread Nutella on each slice and spoon berries on top. Enjoy this sweet treat!

CARNEVALE
VENICE

Italy enjoys many holidays throughout the year. Celebrations often mark religious holidays. Each Italian town celebrates the day dedicated to its **patron saint**. Catholic holy days like Christmas and Easter are major holidays. The festival before Lent is called *Carnevale*. People go to parties and parades wearing fancy masks and costumes.

Italy's national holiday is Republic Day on June 2. The Italian Air Force flies over Rome. The planes trail green, white, and red smoke. Communities across Italy hold festivals celebrating their local foods and culture. Strolling through ancient piazzas and eating delicious treats in the sunshine makes for a perfect Italian day!

REPUBLIC DAY
ROME

79 CE
Mount Vesuvius erupts, burying the city of Pompeii in ash

509 BCE
Romans overthrow the ruling Etruscans and form the Roman Republic

1498
Leonardo da Vinci completes *The Last Supper*, one of the greatest Renaissance paintings

476
The Roman Empire falls due to attacks and the rise of Christianity

46-44 BCE
Julius Caesar becomes Rome's Emperor and rules the Italian peninsula and beyond

1300s
City-states including Genoa and Florence act as independent countries, while popes control the southern part of the peninsula

1861
Italy becomes unified under King Victor Emmanuel II

1946
Italians vote to become a republic

1993
Italy is one of the founding members of the European Union

1922
Benito Mussolini becomes prime minister of Italy and takes complete control of the government within a few years

1940
Italy enters World War II as an ally to Germany and Japan

2006
Turin hosts the Winter Olympics, and Italy wins the soccer World Cup

ITALY FACTS

Official Name: Italian Republic

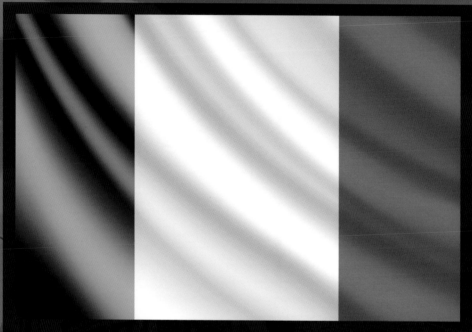

Flag of Italy: Italy's flag is a tricolor design of three vertical stripes inspired by the French revolution flag. The green, white, and red stripes came from the Milan city militia.

Area: 116,348 square miles
(301,340 square kilometers)

Capital City: Rome

Important Cities: Milan, Naples, Venice, Florence, Turin, Palermo

Population:
62,007,540 (July 2016)

WHERE PEOPLE LIVE

COUNTRYSIDE
31%

CITY
69%

MANUFACTURING
28.3%

FARMING
3.9%

JOBS

SERVICES
67.8%

Main Exports:

clothing   textiles   chemicals

food   beverages   motor vehicles

National Holiday:
Republic Day (June 2)

Main Language:
Italian

Form of Government:
parliamentary republic

Title for Country Leaders:
president, prime minister

RELIGION

NONE
17%

OTHER
1%

MUSLIM
2%

CHRISTIAN
80%

Unit of Money:
Euro; 100 cents make up 1 Euro.

GLOSSARY

amphitheater—a round, open-air building with tiered rows of seats surrounding a central performance space

cuisine—a style of cooking

gelato—soft, rich Italian ice cream

gladiators—people who fought for others' entertainment in ancient Rome

heritage—the traditions, achievements, and beliefs that are part of the history of a group of people

lagoons—shallow bodies of water that connect to larger bodies of water

native—originally from the area or related to a group of people that began in the area

patron saint—a saint who is believed to look after a country or group of people

peninsula—a section of land that extends out from a larger piece of land and is almost completely surrounded by water

plain—a large area of flat land

service jobs—jobs that perform tasks for people or businesses

temperate—associated with a mild climate that does not have extreme heat or cold

terrain—the surface features of an area of land

tiered—arranged in a series of rows that rise above one another

tourists—people who travel to visit another place

volcanoes—holes in the earth; when a volcano erupts, hot ash, gas, or melted rock called lava shoots out.

World Cup—an international soccer competition held every four years; the World Cup is the world's largest soccer tournament.

TO LEARN MORE

AT THE LIBRARY

James, Simon. *Ancient Rome*. New York, N.Y.: DK Children, 2015.

Morganelli, Adrianna. *Cultural Traditions in Italy*. New York, N.Y.: Crabtree Publishing Company, 2016.

Savery, Annabel. *Italy*. Mankato, Minn.: Smart Apple Media, 2012.

ON THE WEB

Learning more about Italy is as easy as 1, 2, 3.

1. Go to www.factsurfer.com.

2. Enter "Italy" into the search box.

3. Click the "Surf" button and you will see a list of related web sites.

With factsurfer.com, finding more information is just a click away.

INDEX